Internet Marketing Basics for Business Owners

How to Survive Owning a Business in a Digital World

Mike Balistreri

Mike Balistreri – Internet Basics for Business Owners © 2012

Author Self Published

(mikeb@getFound.us)

ALL RIGHTS RESERVED. This book contains material protected under International and Federal Copyright Laws and Treaties. Any unauthorized reprint or use of this material is prohibited. No part of this book may be reproduced or transmitted in any form or by any means, electronic or mechanical, including photocopying, recording, or by any information storage and retrieval system without express written permission from the author / publisher.

Original Publishing Date 5/1/2012

Revised 8/30/2016

How to Survive Owning a Business in a Digital World

Intro

As a business owner most of my life, I understand the trials, tribulations and the challenges faced when trying to keep a business vibrant and successful over time.

For better or worse, the Internet has changed the global, and more significantly, the local market place for many businesses.

Days of having a nice ad in the Yellow Pages and reaping the rewards are over. The Internet is the new Yellow Pages, if you don't exist there, to most consumers, you don't exist at all.

This book is my attempt to help the business owner to understand what is needed to protect market share and thrive in this environment.

*Stats – Google will receive more than 3 billion searches, which averages to the 54,000 queries a second – that is over 90 billion each month and about **1.2 trillion** a year worldwide.*
Daily Mail June 27, 2016

Why Internet Marketing is Important

Here is a shock, not all companies need Internet marketing. Companies that sell to other businesses may not need to get found on the Internet. Most of these companies rely on target customers, sales calls, relationship building and other means to make their sales numbers. Of course, even these companies need a website and the ability for customers to find their phone number, address, product info and other details on the web.

For companies that sell to consumers, Internet marketing and Search Engine Optimization (SEO) is usually essential for survival.

Over 80% of consumers rely on the Internet to find phone numbers and addresses for local businesses.

When searching for a business, consumers are bombarded with a number of third party sites. Ads from Google and aggregator sites like Google Plus, Yelp, Superpages, Yellow Pages, etc... tend to show up before most company's websites. This is not good for the company or the consumers. These sites will show ads for competitors and both good and bad reviews. They will also see search results from competitors.

There are companies with business models that are based entirely on stealing traffic and customers from businesses. It is the Wild West out there and businesses are in a high noon showdown for their lives.

Countless companies have been ruined by unscrupulous Internet hackers, scoundrels and outright bastards. It is incredibly important for a company to protect its current customer relationships, or the company will watch their market share disappear.

The great news is that it is not only possible to protect your current customers, but also to get new customers from the Internet.

Protecting Market Share
When it comes to protecting a company on the Internet, an aggressive and strategic plan is required. The main threats to a company's market share are stolen traffic, fraudulent behavior and reputation damage.

Stolen Traffic
A web searcher that is using the Internet to find a company that is already known to them usually types the name of the company in a search engine like Google.

Google then returns results. In these results are paid advertising at the top and to the right of the screen. Hopefully, the company being searched for has their website, Google Places, and other sites displayed on the first page of search results.

Usually some of the first page results are competitors. So, just by the surfer entering the name of the company in a search, he now is exposed to special advertisements and competitors' websites and Google Places. This is the first opportunity for that precious traffic to be stolen.

Think of the Internet as a freeway. As people are driving to the company's store, they are seeing billboards and neon signs for other companies. The result is some of the cars (traffic) driving to the store are now taking off ramps before they get to the store.

If aggregator sites like Google Plus, Yelp, Superpages or Yellow Pages are coming up on the search, a second opportunity to have traffic stolen exists.

These sites use a company's name to drive traffic to *their* websites. Once a visitor hits the website, he is bombarded with ads from the company's competitors and often even negative reviews about your company.

Lost Internet search traffic turns into lost customers.

Case Study – "I was in a sales call with a local Ace Hardware store. Upon doing searches for their name, one of the first results that came up was their Superpages listing. They were happy to see it on the first page. We then clicked on the link; SuperPages opened and had a nice listing for the Ace Hardware and a map to the right of the listing. Once again, they were happy. Something didn't look quite right; however, I noticed that the map was not of their location, it was a map to the location of their biggest competitor a mile from their store. At the bottom of the map, in tiny, tiny type was the name of the competitor. This was a paid ad for the competition and could not be changed. Now they were not so happy. They employed my company to create a search environment that pushed their Superpages listing down to the second results page."

Much Internet traffic is lost at this point, but there are more threats. Some websites use fraudulent practices in order to steal market share.

Fraudulent Practices

There are bad apples everywhere, but the Internet seems to have orchards of them. Unfortunately, it is very easy and lucrative to steal market share with fraud.

Some of the fraudulent techniques that are used to steal traffic are fake Google, Yahoo and Bing local accounts, hacking sensitive client data and fake reviews.

Competitors will create Google, Yahoo and Bing local accounts using a different company's name, but their company's address, website and phone number. This is pretty easy to do and can cause a lot of damage. Unfortunately, it is also profitable for the bad apples.

Companies should periodically search their name to make sure this is not happening. It is usually pretty easy to get the account updated or cancelled.

Some companies are able to find email addresses for a competing company's customer data base. This could be the result of hacking or from a poorly structured email from the company.

In either case, the new company bombards the customer base with emails, special offers, etc… maybe even an email stating that the company was sold or out of business.

Once again, lost customers are the result. A company must treat their customer data as golden and protect it through state of the art software.

Online reputation can be either a great competitive edge or a catastrophe for a consumer company. Many times fake, negative reviews are posted by competitors.

When this happens, it is hard to recover. The review site usually has a process for business owners to dispute bad reviews. Companies need to know the process and use it.

The best thing that a company can do is to have happy customers post as many positive reviews as possible to combat the negative ones.

Case Study – "I typed my insurance agent's name in a Google search. To my surprise, a Google Places account came up with an address a block from my office, I knew my agent, Mike's, office to be about 5 miles away. I called the number listed and asked for "Mike". The man said that his name was Bill and that he could help me with whatever Mike could. I hung up and dug out Mike's card. I gave him a call and together we learned that a State Farm colleague used Mike's name to create a fake Google Places to steal his customers."

Increasing Sales

The great news is that companies cannot only protect market share, but actually increase sales through Internet marketing.

There are many ways to increase sales through the Internet. Some ways are increased traffic, increased conversion of visitors to prospects and ecommerce.

The majority of topics in this book deal with increasing website traffic. In most cases, more web traffic results in more leads and more leads result in more sales.

If a company doubles the number of leads (traffic) and maintains status quo close rate, sales will double. If the company also doubles the close ratio (conversions), now the company has increased sales 400%!

Some companies just need to create an online store to increase sales dramatically.

A good SEO strategy also includes constant and predictable customer communication, increasing sales per customer is also a good source of increased total sales. This can be done through email, special Internet only offers, etc...

Prospect and Customer Communication

Most of us have filled out a form that asked for our work phone number, home phone number, cell phone number, address and email. Sometimes there was a box to indicate which communication method was preferred.

In today's world, that same form exists, but now it includes Facebook, blog, text, Twitter, Instant Message, online chat, interactive website, etc... to ignore the preferred communication method risks losing the customer.

For example, imagine if the company's policy was to only communicate in person and did not offer phone calls or email. This is the same as not using social media today.

Every consumer sales company should have an active blog, Facebook fan page and Twitter account.

A great way to understand how a company can use these communication tools is to check out Starbucks social media accounts.

Usually, the best way to get started in this area is to first use it personally. *If you have them, a great way to get started is to ask your kids how to use them!*

Search Engine Optimization

The process of protecting your market share and increasing your sales through Internet marketing and search engine relevance is generally called SEO, which is an abbreviation for Search Engine Optimization.

Some people feel that this only involves a website being found on a Google search, but it is much more than that. There are many, many search engines that can affect a company's success. Some of these search engines are:

Google
Bing
Yahoo
Google Places
Bing Local
Yahoo Local
Yelp
Instagram
Pinterest
LinkedIn
Angie's List
Craigslist
YouTube
Facebook
Twitter
MySpace
WordPress
Tumblr

Superpages

Yellow Pages

Google Plus

Merchant Circle

SlideShare

This is just a short list, it is estimated that there are over 500 search engines used in North America.

Since Google is by far the most popular search engine, most people base their SEO efforts on that search engine.

There are many components that combine to form a comprehensive SEO strategy. This book will address the most important of these areas.

The first deals only with a company's website, it is called Organic SEO.

Organic SEO

Organic SEO is the process of manipulating a website for increasing the chance that is found, crawled and indexed by search engines in the most comprehensive method available.

The goal of organic SEO is to have a website show in the free results area of a search engine results page, as high on the page as possible.

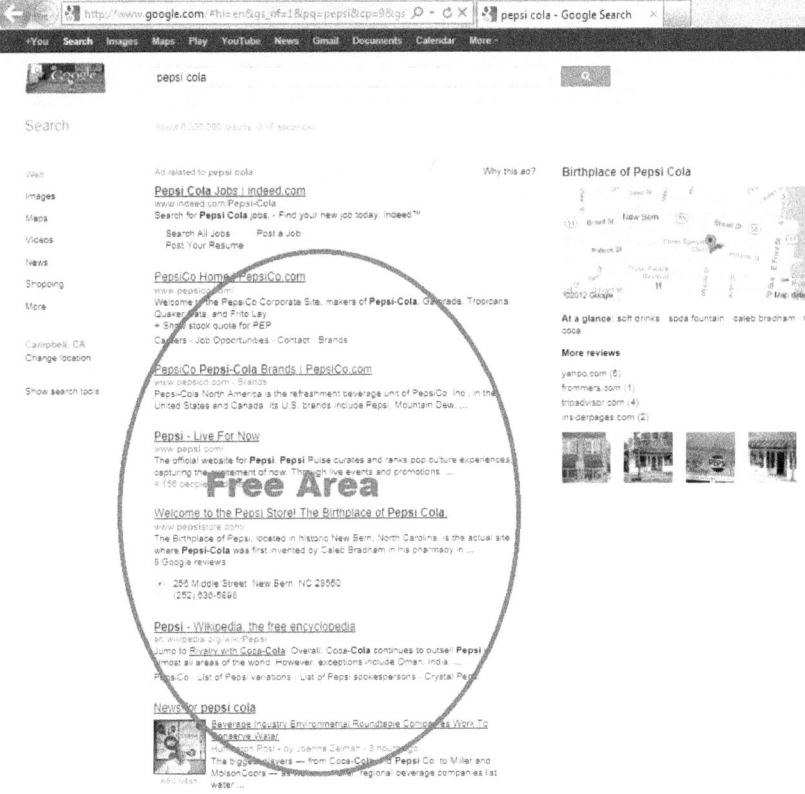

The results above and to the right of the free area are paid advertising on a per click basis.

Placement in the top portion of the results page is critical. Studies show that up to 66% of Internet users make a choice of next action without ever scrolling down the page.

Organic SEO results include websites, social media accounts, videos, places, maps and local accounts.

A website should be created and modified with Google in mind. The challenge is to make it as easy as possible for Google to understand what a company does and why they should send their search users to that site.

How do search engines work? What are they looking for in a highly relevant search website? That is the million dollar question. Search engine companies such as Google, vigorously defend their proprietary information and search algorithms.

Through experience, trial and error and experimentation, some things that they look for are pretty much general knowledge.

Search engines review websites on a regular basis, usually the frequency of review is based on the amount of raw visitor traffic that a website has in a period. The process of reviewing the sites is referred to as "crawling".

A search engine "crawler" is an automated software program that processes a website's source code and looks for items that it recognizes. It then takes these items and puts them in a database. This process is called "indexing".

A large number of indexed pages in a search engine database is an important factor in search relevancy. Some of the items that are stored in the database are:
Page Content
Inbound Links
Page Titles
Page Descriptions
Keywords / Meta Tags
This book will now address these items.

Page Content
Page content are the words, images, links, etc… that are visible to a visitor on a website's pages. Search engines will grade the content from elementary school to graduate school in complexity.

In general, it is better to have the lowest possible complexity so that the search engine is confident that any web searcher they send to your site will understand and be able to use the content.

An easy to use and navigate website usually is what a search engine views as positive. Complex site maps and architecture is generally a negative.

Inbound Links
One factor that gives search engines confidence in returning a website in a search result is the number of relevant websites that link it.

In the past, this was generally accepted as the most important factor. Many SEO service companies specialized in link building. These companies would link any website to another website. They are generally referred to as "link farms".

Partly due to these companies success, the importance of inbound links has decreased. Websites that link to each other will have those links ignored; these are called "reciprocal links". Search engines no longer only look at the overall number of links a website may have, but now weigh relevant links.

Search engines look at links from quality sites that are relevant to the site that is receiving the link. The more relevant and respected the link, the better. Having many relevant links is a huge positive for most search engines.

Page Titles / Page Descriptions / Keywords / Meta Tags

In order to have good search engine relevancy, a company needs to communicate what products and services it provides to search engines. The main method of doing this is to put the information on each page of a website.

It is possible to add programming code to the underlying script for every website page. By adding lines of code that reference nomenclature that search engines understand, a company can basically tell Google what the relevant search terms are for their website.

Here is an example of the code from Pepsi's website:

<meta name="description" content="The official website for Pepsi. Pepsi Pulse curates and ranks pop culture experiences, capturing the excitement of now. Through live events and promotions, people are invited to participate and share their own Live For Now moments." />
<meta name="keywords" content="pepsi, pepsico, pepsi beverages, diet pepsi, pepsi max, pepsi next, pepsi pulse, pepsi ads, live for now, live4now, now moment, now, vive hoy, mi pepsi, hoy, pop, soda,

beverage, drink, refreshing, thirsty, refresh" />
<meta name="title" content="Pepsi - Live For Now" />

Pepsi is telling Google that it would be appropriate to show their website in the search results for the words "pepsi, pepsico, pepsi beverages, diet pepsi, pepsi max, pepsi next, pepsi pulse, pepsi ads, live for now, live4now, now moment, now, vive hoy, mi pepsi, hoy, pop, soda, beverage, drink, refreshing, thirsty, refresh". Of course, getting on the search results page is not guaranteed, but without this code, it may never happen.

Note – It is easy to see what page titles, page descriptions and keywords are being employed by a website. From Internet Explorer, click on the gear symbol at the top right of the page, then choose "developer tools".

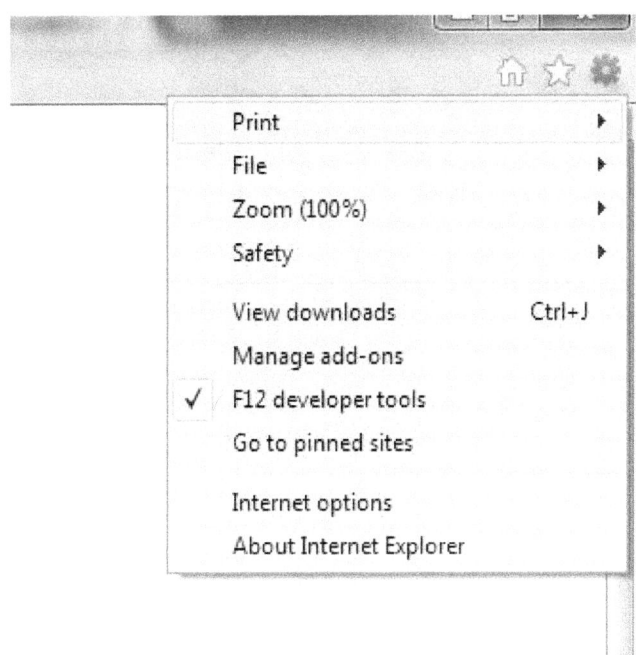

A new window will then open, click on the "script" tab.

```
 Pepsi - Live For Now - F12
File  Find  Disable  View  Images  Cache  Tools  Validate  | Browser M
HTML   CSS   Console  Script  Profiler  Network
                             www.pepsi.com
  1  <!DOCTYPE html>
  2  <!--[if lt IE 7]> <html debug="true" lang="en" cl
  3  <!--[if IE 7]>    <html debug="true" lang="en" cl
  4  <!--[if IE 8]>    <html debug="true" lang="en" cl
  5  <!--[if gt IE 8]><!-->
  6  <html lang="en" class="no-js" xmlns:fb="http://ww
  7  <!--<![endif]-->
  8  <head >
  9  <meta http-equiv="X-UA-Compatible" content="IE=Em
 10  <!-- <script type="text/javascript" src="https://
 11
 12  <meta http-equiv="Content-Type" content="text/htm
 13  <meta name="description" content="The official we
 14  <meta name="keywords" content="pepsi, pepsico, pe
 15  <meta name="title" content="Pepsi - Live For Now"
 16  <title>Pepsi - Live For Now</title>
```

It is pretty easy to find the code, it is usually in the first 25 lines. While this is a great tool for companies to research competition, it is also a great tool for their competition to do research on them.

Local Search

Companies that sell to consumers in a geographic area surrounding their business location need to include local search strategies in their organic SEO plan.

In the simplest form this process is based on creating, optimizing and maintaining accounts on the following platforms:

Google Places

Yahoo! Local

Bing Local

Yelp

Depending on a company's geographic region, industry, product and/or service type other accounts may need to be created, optimized and maintained on these platforms:

Craigslist

Instagram

Pinterest

Angie's List

Merchant Circle

CitySearch

Superpages

HealthGrades

This is just a short list. There are also usually geographic local community sites and government sites.

Google Places, Yahoo! Local and Bing Local

Local maps sites can drive a lot of traffic and sales to a local company. These sites require a company to claim their site, verify identity through the mail or via a phone call.

These sites also allow companies to add keywords, photos, links, and videos to an account. They usually have great keyword relevancy and are a good way to get a business on the first page of search results.

Local map sites are preferred by a majority of Internet users and this trend should continue to grow with many communities sponsoring "buy local" campaigns.

Yelp and Other Review Sites

Review sites can be life or death for a company. 87% of online reviews are positive, but the 11% that are negative can have a big impact. Over 88% of consumers say that they have not bought a product or service due to reading a negative online review.

A proper strategy for a company in this area includes a process to make it as easy as possible for a happy customer to post a positive review. A company should also have a comprehensive plan to deal with negative reviews.

The negative review plan should include a standard public response to every negative review that includes an apology, an acknowledgement of the complainant's issues, an offer to make the situation right and a plan for resolution.

A resolution plan may include a refund, exchange, etc... In a large dollar situation, it may also include an offer of arbitration. A company needs to remember that the response is a customer service tool as well as an advertisement to all other users of the website of how the company handles complaints.

Many companies' responses are written with anger, defending the company's position and belittling the complainant. That is not a great message to send to potential clients.

A negative review is not unlike an unhappy customer standing in a retail door way with a sign stating not to do business with the store *and he stands there 24 hours a day*. It is critical that these sites do not tarnish a company's online reputation.

HOW YELP CAN HELP
SMALL BUSINESSES TAKE ADVANTAGE OF RAVE REVIEWS

Yelp can be a scary place for some small businesses, but don't fear the unknown. In reality, just having a presence on the review site can bolster customer awareness and provide small businesses with new customer insights. Here, we look at how small businesses can benefit from consumers' love affair with the review site.

YELP REVIEWS ARE TRUSTED REVIEWS

Consumers consider Yelp a trusted source for reviews and opinions.

72% of consumers trust online reviews as much as personal recommendations.

90% of Yelp users say positive reviews impact their company buying choices.

When deciding what businesses to go to, customers based their choices on:

- Text Reviews **44%**
- Business Ratings **26%**
- Quantity of Reviews **17%**
- Reviews from Friends or Family **14%**

YELP = PURCHASES

Yelp is a powerful deciding factor for many consumers. Reviews and ratings heavily inform where and what they choose to purchase.

93% of people who conduct research on review sites typically make purchases at the businesses they look up.

Top Business Types Regularly Searched on Yelp:

78%	65%	63%	60%	57%	51%	48%	43%	42%	40%	35%	32%	30%	25%
Restaurants	Beauty and Spa	Food	Nightlife	Home Local Services	Professional Services	Shopping	Pets	Hotels and Travel	Auto	Arts and Entertainment	Health and Medical	Real Estate	Financial Services

SMALL BUSINESSES, BIG BENEFITS

Small businesses are taking note of the rise in consumer demand for online information. Today, 66% of small businesses spend more time on social media sites, compared to a year ago.

Based on a 2012 survey by Vertical Response:

- **90%** were on Facebook
- **70%** were on Twitter

This general rise in social media use has enabled more small businesses to attract customers based solely on recommendations.

YELP = $$

According to a recent survey conducted by Boston Consulting Group, small businesses that took advantage of Yelp business accounts saw an increase in annual revenue.

$8,000 Average increase in annual revenue for small businesses with Yelp accounts.

$23,000 Average increase in annual revenue for small business that paid to advertise on Yelp.

REACH FOR THE STARS: THEY MAKE A DIFFERENCE

A research team at UC Berkeley discovered that a restaurant's chance of selling out during peak dining times jumps from 13% to 34% when increased from 3 to 3.5 stars. Those stats climb another 30% when recommendations hit 4 stars.

Restaurant's chance of selling out:
- ★★★ 13%
- ★★★½ 34%
- ★★★★ 35%

CHANGING THE WAY SMALL BUSINESS DOES BUSINESS

In addition to increasing revenue, a March 2013 Merchant Warehouse survey of 812 small businesses found that many companies are seeing increased customer awareness since joining Yelp.

77% of small businesses that use Yelp say the site has changed the way they respond to customer issues and complaints.

With this kind of free crowdsourcing, small businesses can gauge what their customers want for free.

HOWEVER,
MERCHANT WAREHOUSE FOUND THAT NOT EVERYONE IS TAKING ADVANTAGE OF THE REVIEW SITE'S OPPORTUNITIES

87% of small businesses surveyed don't actively use review sites like Yelp.

22% of small businesses with Yelp pages have never actually looked at their pages at all.

Review sites like Yelp pose big growth opportunities for small businesses that use them strategically. Consumer demand for online reviews and recommendations can mean huge benefits for small businesses that present even a small level of online presence to interact with customers, build customer awareness, promote their brands, and engage in customer conflict resolution — all for free.

WHY NOT TAKE ADVANTAGE?

Merchant Warehouse

YouTube and other Video Sites

YouTube is the second largest search engine in the world. It is a great platform for posting information and branding your company.

When a video is posted on YouTube, it is possible to name the video, create a description and attached keywords with SEO and organic search in mind.

It is a great opportunity to receive search results and distribute information. Most companies would benefit from filming a short video and putting it on their YouTube channel.

The importance of video sites really varies with the company's industry, product or service. But, since it is relatively easy to create and update, every company should have a YouTube channel.

- *Stats – YouTube has over a billion users — almost one-third of all people on the Internet — and every day people watch hundreds of millions of hours on YouTube and generate billions of views.*
- *YouTube overall, and even YouTube on mobile alone, reaches more 18-34 and 18-49 year-olds than any cable network in the U.S.*

YouTube, August 2016

Blogs, Facebook, Twitter and other Social Marketing

Search engines like to see active social media from a company when determining search relevancy. The search engines look at the accounts and analyze them.

In most cases it is worse for search engines to see an account that is not used than not to see an account at all. This is also true for Internet surfers.

So, companies must, at a minimum, create a blog, Facebook and Twitter account and must update each account 10 times per month.

That amount of activity should pass the necessary evil requirement; however, not using these accounts as communication tools is a mistake.

About 79% of businesses have a Facebook page, 59% are on Twitter, 39% have a blog and 33% have a YouTube account. Most of these accounts are never used. This gives a huge advantage to companies that do use them.

Customers want communication on social platforms. Companies that embrace this technology increase sales.

They use Facebook to share pictures, news, specials, videos, anecdotes, run contests and announce product releases. A company can also dialogue with customers on the platform.

- Huge Member Base - Over 1 Billion Monthly Active Facebook Users
- 93% of Consumers Research Products Online
- Free Marketing Channel – Your Posts Show Up in Members News Feed
- Leverage Your Website on the Corporate Website with a Link for Fans
- Incredibly Targeted, Inexpensive Ad Programs – Build Fans by Region, Age, Gender, Marital Status, Interests
- Communicate Sales, Home Shows, Personnel
- Facebook Users are 76% Female
- Average User Spends 40 Minutes a Day
- 49% of Consumers Like a Facebook Page to Support the Brand

Reasons for Becoming a Brand Fan on Facebook

QUESTION: The following are the reasons of becoming a fan that were mentioned to us by others. Which, if any, of the following reasons led you to become a Fan or "Like" the following brands on Facebook?

49%	To support the brand I like	27%	To share my interests / lifestyle with others
42%	To get a coupon or discount	21%	To research brands when I was looking for specific products / services
41%	To receive regular updates from brands I like	20%	Seeing my friends are already a fan or "liked"
35%	To participate in contests	18%	A brand advertisement (TV, online, magazine) led me to fan the brand
31%	To share my personal good experiences	15%	Someone recommended me to fan the brand

Source: Syncapse.com

Twitter can be used to post more immediate news. Since the characters are limited to 141 characters, it is also a great place to post links to websites, landing pages, etc...

A blog is a great place to post information that requires more content. It is similar to a newsletter, except the communication can be daily. Blogs can also be searched for previous posts, so it can be a good data base of information about a company, product or service.

For most of these services, 100 fans, followers, subscribers, etc. is the magic number. Search relevance usually increases for each of these services after the number of interactions is achieved.

Pay Per Click

Google is worth billions due to one revenue source, pay per click (PPC) advertising. Companies regularly pay over $10.00 for one click on their ad.

Pay per click is based on keywords and is sold based on either a number of impressions or the number of clicks on an advertisement.

This is a targeted way to drive traffic and create leads. However, it may be very hard to achieve a positive return on investment (ROI) due to high cost.

Pay per click advertising is offered by many websites, including Facebook and LinkedIn.

Inclusion of pay per click advertising in an SEO plan is really dependent on a company's average profit margin per sale and the corresponding ROI.

Groupon and other Deals of the Day Advertising

One of the fastest growing sales models on the Internet are the daily deal sites. Groupon is the most famous, but there are many others.

Living Social, Plum District, etc... offer a daily email and Internet offer. Many companies use these deals in an attempt to grow their sales.

The truth is that they are a great deal for the daily deal company, but not the company offering the product or service.

It is common for the daily deal to be 50% off of the normal retail price. The 50% sale is then split between the daily deal company and the company making the offer.

This means that the company offering the product and service receives of 25% of their normal retail price. The daily deal company gets the same money, but does not have the cost of delivering the product or service.

The providing company takes the risk based on a few reasons. One is that they will get a pretty big lump sum sale; others are that they now get an influx of new business and new customers. They also are told that the vast majority of purchasers will not use the offer before the expiration date.

The truth is that most companies go through the same process. They are usually overwhelmed by the response and have a huge problem delivering the offer.

When consumers do redeem the offer, they seldom turn into repeat customers. They are much more likely to wait for the next company offering a daily deal. These consumers rarely are loyal to any brand or company.

Since the company has issues delivering, it is true that they have sold something for nothing in many cases. One reason for expiration is that the consumers just cannot schedule the service offered in the deal and the offers not redeemed are pure profit.

They can't hire more people, because they profit margin has been reduced by selling it at 25% of retail. This leads to the true problem with these deals.

The providing company ends up with many upset customers. Upset customers on the Internet lead to negative reviews on Yelp and other review sites.

Now the company that started this process to increase sales faces a situation in which they lose sales due to an eroded online reputation.

All that being said, there are some companies that are able to use these sites to deliver product and services that result in profitable sales.

E-commerce

Online shopping is expected to burgeon past the $1.5 trillion marker this year in worldwide sales – with some experts predicting that ecommerce will surpass $2 trillion in the next few years – it's the fastest growing and one of the most valuable industries.

These sales can be made on a company's website or a number of other sites, some run by the company and some that just sell without involving the company.

Ebay is one example of a do it yourself site. Sites like O.com sell product without the company needing to participate in the sales cycle.

Most companies that sell a product or service should offer an online purchase option to its customers. It is usually not a huge project to add an online store to a website.

One great thing about the store is that it operates 24 hours a day, 7 days per week. The store can replace a salesperson. Many companies offer a discount for online sales, especially if it means that they do not have to pay a salesperson's commission on that sale.

Google Analytics

The basis of all SEO work should be Google Analytics analysis. Google Analytics is a great tool for measuring and analyzing the traffic coming to a website.

Some basic metrics are:

Visits

Unique Visitors

New Visits

Bounce Rate

Pagesviews

Pages per Visit

Average Time on Site

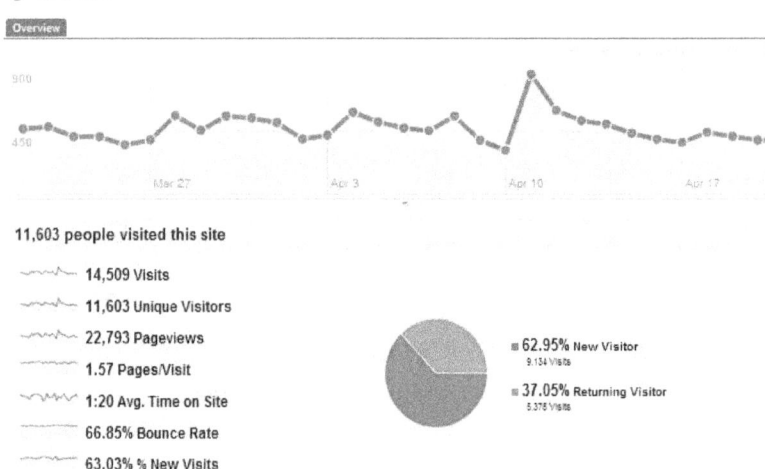

By tracking and analyzing these metrics, a company can determine how well their site is performing, their conversion rate and can strategically plan for improvement. The conversion rate is the number of actions such as emails, chat, phone calls, forms, etc. divided by the total Visits.

There are whole books written about Google Analytics. Analytics are the life blood of a good SEO strategy. Results must be analyzed and then strategies modified accordingly.

It would take 100s of pages to adequately discuss Google Analytics, so we will just be looking at some of the most important factors.

Visits - The continuous access of a website until a visitor stops accessing the page and/or is inactive for 30 minutes. Several different pages may be accessed in one visit. The time out length is customizable and determined by cookies. Websites vary immensely in the number of visits in a period. Period measurement is usually done in a monthly or last 30 days method.

This metric is most valuable when comparing time periods and analyzing increase or decrease. In general, a healthy website should increase this number about 10% to 30% annually.

Unique Visitors – This is the number of visits from computers that did not have an identifiable cookie for a date range. It can also be described as the number of "First Time" visits for a period. If the computer in question cleared its cookies, it would show as a new visit even though it accessed the site already.

This metric is best used when compared to Visits. If a company has 300 Visits and 200 Unique Visitors, they averaged 1.5 visits per Unique Visitor. This a good measure of engagement with visitors.

A company should have at least a 1.2 Visits/Unique Visitor ratio, but some companies may average 30 or above if the site is accessed daily.

New Visits – This is the number of visits from computers that did not have an identifiable cookie for the website for a certain period. It can also be described as the number of "Truly First Time" visits for the life of a website for a certain period. If the computer in question cleared its cookies, it would show as a new visit even though it accessed the site already.

The number of Unique Visits will always be more than the number of New Visits. New Visits is a subset of Unique Visits.

Many companies track the number of New Visits and feel that is an indicator of website lead generation performance. Most websites average of 60% New Visits.

Notes on Visitors – Remember that these numbers may not be accurate due to being based on computer cookies. Also, these metrics do not account for multiple users on one computer.

Bounce Rate – When a visit consists of only one page, whether that is the home page or a sub page, it is considered a Bounce. The number of Bounces divided by the total Visits is the Bounce Rate.

In general, websites average about a 40% Bounce Rate, but they vary a lot. A Bounce Rate of 80% usually means that the website has big problems with engagement.

As with most of these statistics, there are shades of grey. Many users may have a favorite pizza place's order page or contact page bookmarked for quick access. If the majority of Visitors use the website in this fashion, a high Bounce Rate may not be a problem at all.

This metric is used to measure the success of changes to the user interface pages (usually the home page) or the success of advertising. Increases in Bounce Rates over time without a clear reason are usually a concern and needs investigation.

Pagesviews and Average Pageviews per Visit – Pageviews are the the total number of times a Visit accesses a web page. If the Visitor uses the back button or refreshes the page it is another Pageview.

This metric is another engagement evaluation tool. Usually, the more Pageviews per Visit, the better, comparing the number over time periods is important.

Most websites average at least 2 Pageviews per visit. Pageviews are better analyzed when the numbers of Bounce visits are subtracted.

For example, if Bounce Rate is 67% and the Total Visits 1,000, only 330 Visitors accessed more than one page. If you subtract the 670 Bounce visits from the Pageviews of 1,500 (830) and divide by the 330 multipage Visitors, the adjusted Bounce Rate is over 2.5 pages instead of the 1.5 pages on the Google Analytic report.

Average Time on Site – This is the time from when a Visit is started (website accessed) until the last page of the visit is accessed. It does not include the time spent on the last page accessed.

Most companies are able to average at least 1.5 minutes per Visit. If the average is under 1 minute, it is usually an indicator of a problem with the website.

Other components are also important to Google Analytic analysis. One great tool allows for easy to viewing and comparing of the Total Visits, Average Time on Site, Pageviews per Visit, New Visitor percentage and Bounce Rate by Visit Source and Visit Keyword.

Comparing these numbers allows a company to determine what Visit Source and Visit Keyword are producing the most valuable website traffic. This is critical if the company is participating in any advertising that results in website visits.

Companies also track the percentage of Visits from Search Traffic, Visits from Referral Traffic, Direct Traffic and from Campaigns.

SEO Goals

A to medium size company should have four goals that are achieved in this order:

1 – Dominate the first page of search results for a search of the company name. At least the first five organic results should be for items that the company controls, i.e. website, website pages, Facebook account, Google Places, YouTube video, Twitter account, blog, etc...

2 – First page presence on the search results page for the company's main product and/or service keywords in a geographic range.

3 – Prospect and customer communication in every communication method preferred by their targeted Internet visitor demographic.

4 – Wise use of the resources spent on SEO and associated efforts.

Conclusion

If you own or manage a business to consumer enterprise, you need to address SEO and Internet marketing.

Make it a habit to search for your company's name and keywords. Make sure to normalize the search to exclude your personal search preferences.

If you need to, employ a SEO company that fits your budget. It is more important that you understand the basic concepts in order to manage and evaluate the success of a company that you employ than to do the work yourself.

After all, you could drive a package 120 miles and deliver it, but you usually send it UPS.

About the Author

Mike Balistreri is the owner of getFound.us, a leading SEO company specializing in companies with a focus on service industries.

He resides in San Jose, CA where he enjoys spending time with his two children, grandchildren and enjoys hiking, golf, tennis and business networking.

You can contact Mike at mikeb@getfound.us

Search Engine (SEO) Glossary

Above the fold (ATF): Originally a newspaper term, above the fold means on the top half of the page. Placing a story above the fold makes it more visible. In Web publishing, in which no fold exists, premium placement generally means toward the top of the page, in a position where visitors don't have to scroll down. Screen resolutions differ, of course, so if you design your page using a resolution of 1280 x 1024, for example, your own fold is way down the page. The higher the resolution, the more material you can put into each "fold" portion of the page, because high resolutions make text and graphics smaller. (In effect, high resolution makes the screen bigger.)

Algorithm: A formula or set of steps for solving a particular problem. To be an algorithm, a set of rules must be unambiguous and have a clear stopping point. Algorithms can be expressed in any language, from natural languages like English or French to programming languages like FORTRAN. We use algorithms every day. For example, a recipe for baking a cake is an algorithm. Most programs, with the exception of some artificial intelligence applications, consist of algorithms. Inventing elegant algorithms-algorithms that are simple and require the fewest steps possible-is one of the principal challenges in programming.

Alt Attribute: XHTML tag that provides alternative text when non-textual elements, typically images, cannot be displayed. The image tag is a very important tag. It directs the browser to either a gif or jpeg file. The browser then displays that image file where the command is placed.

Anchor Text: *See* Link Text

Backlink: A link at another site, leading to your site. Also called an *incoming link*. The number and quality of backlinks represent the most important factor in determining a site's PageRank. The value of any backlink is determined partly by the PageRank of the linking site, which is determined partly by the quality of *its* backlinks, and so on.

Bandwidth: Bandwidth refers to the amount of data that can be transferred from one place to another within a certain amount of time. Digital devices measure bandwidth in bytes per second. The bigger the bandwidth, the faster the data can be transferred.

Blog: A blog (short for "weblog") is a journal that's available on the internet. Updating a blog is referred to as "blogging" and the person keeping the blog is a "blogger". Blogs are usually listed in chronological order, with the most recent entry first. Many blogs are available as RSS feeds, which means they are delivered to a feedreader.

Blogosphere: The term blogosphere describes the information available on blogs and/or the sub-culture of those who create and use blogs. By its nature, the blogosphere tends to be democratic, inclusive, and encourages two-way communication between its participants.

Bridge page: *See* doorway page.

Buzz keyword: Coined by Clinton Cimring in 2006, a buzz keyword is a newly created keyword that usually just became recognized as an auto suggestion in Google and Yahoo!.

Cloud Hosting: Cloud Hosting is web hosting where more than one server is used as a host. This may be in the context of multiple servers in one single location or multiple servers in multiple locations. The benefit of the first option of cloud hosting is that if there is a power outage in one geographic location, the second server would not be affected. The benefit of the second option of cloud hosting would be that server resources can be combined for the same files.

Cloaking: A type of search-engine subterfuge in which an indexed Web page is not shown to visitors who click its link in Google (or another search engine). The cloaking works two ways: Visitor content is cloaked from Google, and Google's indexed content is cloaked from visitors. This serves to give a high PageRank to content that ordinarily would rate a low PageRank. Cloaking is not always illicit. A certain type of cloaking are used to deliver pages tailored to a visitor's ISP (America Online, for example) or specific Web browser.

Congregate Websites: congregate website is a term coined by Clinton Cimring in 1998, which refers to any website that compiles other websites in bulk such as directories or networking websites.

Content Dilution: content dilution is the result of either 1) having too much content on a page that is being optimizer for thereby diluting the keyword densities of keywords that would otherwise be featured or 2) having too many pages on a website and thereby loosing the ability to feature all of them.

Crawler: *See* spider.

CRM: Customer relationship management, or CRM, software is for tracking the traditional sales process including marketing automation, lead generation, sales forecasting, measuring ROIs, etc. Note: Although BatchBook is often referred to as a CRM, it is actually more about managing contact information than sales leads, although it could do both.

Cross linking: Intentionally or unintentionally, cross linking creates large backlink networks among sites that exist in the same domain or are owned by the same entity. Unintentional cross linking happens when a site generates a large number of pages with identical navigation links or when at least two sites mutually link related content. When cross linking is done intentionally, the Webmaster is seeking to raise the PageRank of the involved sites. Excessive cross linking can backfire. If Google decides that the resulting enhanced PageRank is artificial, any or all of the sites might be expelled from the Web index. Innocent cross linking between two related sites is usually not a problem.

Deepbot: The unofficial name for Google's monthly spider. Freshbot is the unofficial name of Google's frequently crawling spider. The official name for both crawlers is Googlebot.

Density: Most search engines look for keyword density. Some will only look at the first 200-400 characters of your site, and count the number of times the keyword appears. Some index a small amount of text from the top, middle, and bottom parts of your web page, and search them for keywords. Generally keyword density should be in the 6-8% range. Simply repeating the keyword will not work because some search engines consider grammar structure in their calculations. For a very competitive keyword you could aim a little higher perhaps targeting a 10% range, but you have to take into consideration the search engine may consider this spamming.

Directory Submissions; The act of supplying a URL to a search engine in an attempt to make a search engine aware of a site or page.

Domain: The first- and second-level address of a Web site. Top-level destinations are defined by the domain extension: .com, .net, .org, .biz, and others. The second level adds a domain name: *yoursite*.com.

Domain name: The second-level domain address that identifies and brands a site, such as google.com and amazon.com.

Domain name registration: The process of taking ownership of a domain name. Registrations are processed by dozens of registrars approved by ICANN (Internet Corporation for Assigned Names and Numbers). The cost of domain ownership is no more than $35 per year. (Hosting the domain's Web site is an additional expense.) Registration takes place online, and the activation of a new domain (or moving a domain from one host to another) generally requires no more than 48 hours.

Doorway page: An entry page to a Web site, sometimes known as a splash page. Doorway pages endure a negative connotation due to illicit techniques that send visitors to an entirely different site than the destination they clicked in Google.

Dynamic content: Web pages generated by an in-site process that depends on input from the visitor. Most dynamic content comes from a database operating behind the scenes, feeding information to a Web page created in response to a visitor's query. Search engines are among the largest producers of dynamic content; every Google results page, for example, is pulled from the background index in response to a keyword query. Google's spider generally avoids portions of sites that rely on dynamic page-generation, making it difficult to index the content of those sites.

Entry page: *See* doorway page.

Feed reader: A feed reader (also known as an RSS reader, news reader, or feed aggregator) is an application (desktop or web-based) that allows you to subscribe to multiple RSS feeds, allowing you to read the content from many websites from one place.

Folksonomy: The word folksonomy is a combination of folks, meaning "people", and -onomy, meaning "management". Users create informal social Specials using tags to organize content so that others may easily find and share it.

Forum: A forum is a web-based application that allows people to hold discussions through individual posts. The posts will be displayed in chronological order or as threaded discussions.

Fresh crawl: Google's frequent scan of Web content that occurs between the deep monthly crawls. Google does not publicize the schedule of its intermediate crawls or its target sites. The term "fresh crawl" is an unofficial one used by Webmasters, site optimizers, and other Google obsessive's.

Freshbot: The unofficial name for Google's near-daily spider. Deepbot is the unofficial name of Google's monthly-crawling spider. The official name for both crawlers is Googlebot.

Geo-targeting: Geo-targeting applied to organic SEO is the process of combining keywords with geographic criteria such as city names, metropolitan areas, or zip codes. An example may be, "personal trainer boca raton." These results would appear on the left-hand side of the screen. Geo-targeting applied to SEM is displaying ads based on the target audiences' IP Address. In this case, the searcher would type in, "personal trainer," and the results would appear on the right hand side for searchers who live in zip codes within Boca Raton or the surrounding area.

Googlebot: Google's Web spider.

Heading Tag: Headings (h1-h6) are used as the topics of the website's sections.

Example: <h1>Heading tag</h1>

HTTP: HTTP is called a stateless protocol because each command is executed independently, without any knowledge of the commands that came before it. This is the main reason that it is difficult to implement Web sites that react intelligently to user input. This shortcoming of HTTP is being addressed in a number of new technologies, including ActiveX, Java, JavaScript and cookies. Short for Hypertext Transfer Protocol, the underlying protocol used by the World Wide Web. HTTP defines how messages are formatted and transmitted, and what actions Web servers and browsers should take in response to various commands. For example, when you enter a URL in your browser, this actually sends an HTTP command to the Web server directing it to fetch and transmit the requested Web page.

Incoming/Inbound link: *See* backlink.

Index: In the context of Google, the index is the database of Web content gathered by the Google spider. When Google receives a search query, it matches the query keywords against the index.

Internet Marketing: Internet marketing is the act of promoting products and services by increasing a web site's online visibility. Some of these promotion techniques includes: natural SEO, pay per click advertising, e-mail marketing, newsletter distribution, blogging, community forums, article writing and distribution, and banner advertising.

IP Address: Short for "internet protocol address", this is a unique number that identifies a computer connected to the Internet to other Internet hosts. An example of an IP address is 127.0.0.1.

Keyword: As an optimization term, a keyword represents a core concept of a site or a page. The site's content, XHTML tagging, and layout strategies are based on effective deployment of keywords, which could also be key phrases. Google matches search results to keywords entered by its users and assigns a PageRank in part on how consistently a site presents its keywords.

Keyword Count, Occurrence: How often a keyword or keyword phrase occurs in a particular XHTML page section. The key word count is used is used in a calculation determine the key word density.

Keyword density: A proportional measurement of keywords embedded in a page's content. High keyword density focuses the page's subject in a way that Google's spider understands. The spider can interpret too high a density as spam, which results in a lower PageRank or elimination from the index. Most optimization specialists recommend a density between 5 and 15 percent.

Keyword stuffing: The attempt to gain a higher PageRank (or higher ranking in any search engine) by loading a page's XHTML code or text with keywords. In most cases a visitor can't see the keywords because they're buried in XHTML tags, camouflaged against the background color of the page, or reduced to a tiny typeface. Keyword stuffing violates Google's guidelines for Webmasters and can result in expulsion from the index.

Link farm: A site whose only function is to display outgoing links to participating Web sites. Link farms are disreputable versions of legitimate, topical link exchange sites through which visitors gain some content value. Link farms often have no topicality and present no guidelines or standards of submission. Google does not explicitly threaten expulsion for joining link farms, but it discourages their use.

Link Popularity: a measure of the quantity and quality of sites that link to your site. A growing number of search engines use link popularity in their ranking algorithms. Google uses it as its most important factor in ranking sites. HotBot, AltaVista, Microsoft Bing, Inktomi, and others also use link popularity in their formulas.

Eventually every major engine will use link popularity, so developing and maintaining it are essential to your search engine placement.

Link Text or Anchor Text: Link text is the clickable text which connects one web page to another.

Example: <a href="page.html">link text or anchor text</a>

Local Internet Marketing: Internet marketing geo-targeted through directories, Google maps, and social networking sites.

Geotargeted SEO: SEO targeted toward a city, state, or metropolitan area by utilizing either GEO-Targeted terms and keywords in content or jargon for that specific area.

Manual Submission: adding a URL to the search engines individually by hand.

Meta tag: Positioned near the top of an XHTML document, the meta tag defines basic identifying characteristics of a Web page. Often, several meta tags are used on each page. In those tags you set the page's title, description, and keywords.

Mirror site: Mirror sites duplicate content and are used for both legitimate and engine-spamming purposes. Legitimate mirror sites assist in downloading when a great deal of traffic is trying to reach a page or acquire a file. Illicit mirror sites attempt to fill a search results page with multiple destinations owned by a single entity. When Google discovers a mirror site whose only purpose is to dominate a search page, that site risks expulsion.

Natural SEO: *See* organic seo

Online Advertising: see Internet Marketing

One-Way Link: *See* backlink

Optimization: A set of techniques to improve a Web site's presentation to visitors and its stature in a search engine's index. As a specific field, SEO has suffered in reputation due to unscrupulous individuals and companies using tactics that degrade the integrity of search results and violate guidelines set by those engines. Generally, any optimization scheme that tricks a search engine also tricks visitors to that site, making online life worse for

SEO is reducing the ranking or placement of results like negative press in a search engine by optimizing other pages for the same results. For more on Reverse SEO *See* our <u>Reverse SEO</u> page: http://www.searchenginepartner.com/First-page-placement/reverse-seo.html

Robots.txt file: A simple text file that stops Google (and other search engines that recognize the file and its commands) from crawling the site, selected pages in the site, or selected file types in the site.

RSS feed: RSS stands for Really Simple Syndication. An RSS feed is a document that contains either a summary of content from a web site or the full text of a website. RSS feeds makes it possible for people to keep up with their favorite web sites automatically rather than checking them manually.

SE (search engine): A site, such as Google.com, that matches keywords to Web page content.

SEM (search engine marketing): SEM is SEO that focuses on the marketing aspect of optimization in order to produce results rather than the backend programming, coding, content and design of a website. This marketing is usually associated with pay-per-click campaigns, banner ads, and affiliate networks intended for branding versus action by viewers. The long term results of SEM are usually much higher than organic SEO and may even have a negative return on investment.

SEO: "Strategically Elevating Optimization" is a manipulation of a search engine's algorithm in order to have a website appear higher in a search engine result. For an update See SEO 2.0. It is highly debated in the web community whether the approach was invented by Clinton Cimring or Danny Sullivan of searchengineland.com.

SEO 2.0: SEO 2.0, a term coined by Clinton Cimring in 2006, is an optimization reaction to Google's new Universal algorithm and to Web 2.0 social media sites like Digg, del.icio.us, Technorati, and StumbleUpon. It includes the following results within Google: images, videos, indented pages, subpages, a search within a search, and SML descriptions. For more on SEO 2.0 *See* our <u>SEO 2.0</u> page: http://www.SearchEnginePartner.com/seo-2.0.html

SEO Copywriting: Writing specifically for web pages involves incorporating target keywords that tell the search engines what a specific web page is about. Effective SEO copywriting achieves two goals. 1) It creates persuasive, informative content for the web site visitor while 2) maintaining an optimum keyword count for the search engines to index.

SEO Footprint: An SEO footprint is the imprint a search engine optimizer leaves on the web that can be used to trace his/her activity through various sites. It can be used to locate multiple accounts and multiple sites he/she owns. An SEO footprint is an obvious sign of search engine manipulation and can be used to by Google or competition to rip apart his/her network.

Search Engine Positioning: Typically, a search engine works by sending out a spider to fetch as many documents as possible. Another program, called an indexer, then reads these documents and creates an index based on the words contained in each document. Each search engine uses a proprietary algorithm to create its indices such that, ideally, only meaningful results are returned for each query.

Search Engine Ranking: A program that searches documents for specified keywords and returns a list of the documents where the keywords were found. Although search engine is really a general class of programs, the term is often used to specifically describe systems like Alta Vista and Excite that enable users to search for documents on the World Wide Web and USENET newsgroups

SERP: Search engine results page. A page of links leading to Web pages that match a searcher's keywords.

Server: A server is a computer running administrative software that controls access to the network and its available resources such as printers and disk drives. It also provides resources to computers that are operating on the network. A server can also be a program that contains data or files and that responds to everyone involved. Pure optimization, though, helps everyone: the Webmaster, the search engine, and the visitor. The true values of optimization are clear content, coherent navigation, wide reputation for quality, and high visibility in search engines.

Organic SEO: Organic SEO or Natural SEO is SEO results appearing on the left hand side of a search engine results page. It is distinguishable from SEM which primarily focuses on pay-per-click SEO, which is usually, sponsored links appearing on the right hand side of the screen. Organic SEO usually has a much higher return on investment than SEM; in fact, it usually has the highest ROI out of any advertising or marketing medium.

Outgoing link: A link from your page to another page. Outgoing links don't build PageRank by volume, as incoming links (backlinks) do. However, Google pays attention to the text elements of outgoing links, and a page's optimization can be strengthened by consistent placement of key concepts in that text.

Page redirect: A background link that sends site visitors to another site. Page redirects can be used legitimately, as when a site moves from one domain to another. In that scenario, the Webmaster sensibly keeps the old domain active for a while, seamlessly sending visitors to the new location when they click the old one. As an illicit optimization technique, page redirects deflect visitors from the site indexed by Google to another site that would not be able to gain as high a PageRank. This type of redirect, when uncovered by Google, risks the expulsion of both sites from the index.

PageRank: A proprietary measurement of Google's proprietary ordering of pages in its Web index. PageRank is the most intense point of focus, speculation, observation, and desire in the Webmaster and optimization communities. More than any other single marketing factor, PageRank has the power to determine a site's visibility. A high PageRank moves a page toward the top of any search results page in Google when that page matches the user's keywords. Obtaining a PageRank high enough to break a page into the top ten is the primary goal of Google optimization. An approximate version of any page's PageRank can be checked by displaying the page in Internet Explorer while running the Google Toolbar.

Pixel tracking/web bugs/patty mail: Implementation of a code into the website of the advertiser. This then tracks the user's behavior on the website and reports information back to the adserving system .Pixel tracking is used for Optimization and Tracking conversions.

Prominence: Prominence is the ratio of the position of one keyword or keyword phrase to the positions of the other keywords in an XHTML section of the page. For example in the text enclosed by the BODY tag is one of sections of the page we measure keyword prominence in. Your most important keywords must appear in the crucial locations on your web pages because search engines like pages where keywords appear closer to the top of the page. They should preferable appear in the first paragraphs of your page. Also keep in mind if you include keywords closer to the bottom of your page it will have a negative effect on the overall keyword prominence calculations.

Rank Theft: a term coined by Clinton Cimring in 2001, Rank Theft is a method directories and other congregate websites use to gain the would-be page rank attributed to a website by offering subpages on their own domain. This is different to Google Jacking or spoofing where one website is redirected to another website. Most recently, sites like Myspace and Merchant Circle began offering subpages for free with the hopes that users would use these pages instead of building their own websites. Based on this approach myspace.com's page rank rose approximately 1 point per month. Merchantcircle.com rose from a PR of 0 in 2005 to a PR of 7 in 2008. In contrast, website like wordpress.com and blogger.com offer subdomains rather than subpages in order to avoid these false attributes.

Reverse SEO: a term coined by Clinton Cimring in 2006, Reverse

commands.
Social Media: The term social media describes media that is posed by the user and can take many different forms. Some types of social media are forums, message boards, blogs, wikis and podcasts. Social media applications include Google, Facebook and YouTube.
Social Networking: A social networking site allows you to identify your contacts and establish a link between you and each of your contacts.
Spam: Generally refers to repeated and irrelevant content. As an optimization term, spam refers to loading a page with keywords or loading a search engine's index with mirror sites. Google reacts strongly to spamming, and takes harsh measures against Web sites that use spamming techniques to improve PageRank.
Spider: An automated software program that travels from link to link on the Web, collecting content from Web pages. Spiders assemble this vast collection of content into an index, used by search engines to provide relevant sites to searchers. Spiders are also called crawlers, bots (short for robots), or Web bots. Google's spider appears in Webmaster logs as Googlebot.
Splash page: *See* doorway page.
StopWords: Words that are common in a full-text file but have little value in searching. Words in a stopword file will be excluded from the indexes, considerably reducing the size of the indexes and improving search performance. For example these are stopwords: a, about, an, are, as, at, be, by, com, for, from, how.
Tag: A tag is a keyword used to describe a piece of data (such as a blog post, photo, video, etc.). Tags can either be assigned by the author of the content or the consumer of the content.
Title Tag: XHTML tag used to define the text in the top line of a Web browser, also used by many search engines as the title of search listings.
Title Attribute: Link title is the attribute of the link and adds information about the link, it is rendered as a tool tip in the

browser.

Example: <a href="title-attribute.html" title="link title">text</a>

Trackback: When a blog links to another blog, a trackback is a notification sent between the two blogs letting the receiving blog's author know (s)he is being linked to (this implies that both blogs have the ability to send and receive trackbacks)

Tweet: A "Tweet" is an individual message (or "update") posted from Twitter.

URL: A URL (Universal Resource Locator) is the address of documents and resources on the internet. Most search engines look for the keywords in the domain name, folder name and page name. Keywords should be separated by hyphens.

Example: http://www.keyword1.com/keyword2-keyword3.html **Web 2.0**: Web 2.0 is a trend in the use of World Wide Web technology and web design that aims to facilitate creativity, information sharing, and, most notably, collaboration among users. These concepts have led to the development and evolution of web-based communities and hosted services, such as social-networking sites, wikis, blogs, and folksonomies (the practice of catgorizingcontent through tags). Although the term suggests a new version of the World Wide Web, it does not refer to an update to any technical specifications, but to changes in the ways software developers and end-users use the internet.

Web 3.0:Web 3.0 is a phrase coined by John Markoff of the New York Times in 2006, which refers to a supposed third generation of Internet-based services that collectively comprise what might be called'the intelligent Web'—such as those using semantic web, microformats, natural language search, data-mining, machine learning, recommendation agents, and artificial intelligence technologies—which emphasize machine-facilitated understanding of information in order to provide a more productive and intuitive user experience. Nova Spivack defines Web 3.0 as the third decade of the Web (2010–2020) during which he suggests several major complementary technology trends will reach new levels of maturity simultaneously.

Wiki: A wiki is a website or piece of software that allows users to create and edit webpages. Users are able to link to outside sites and collaborate on the information that is posted.

www.ingramcontent.com/pod-product-compliance
Lightning Source LLC
Chambersburg PA
CBHW061519180526
45171CB00001B/242